Live Canon

2016 Anthology

First Published in 2016
By Live Canon Ltd
www.livecanon.co.uk

© Live Canon 2016

978-1-909703-14-8

Live Canon

2016 Anthology

The poems in this anthology were shortlisted for the
2016 Live Canon International Poetry Prize

Contents

The Diving Horse
Aileen La Tourette

*The Diving Horse performed on the Steel Pier
in Atlantic City, New Jersey, from 1924 until
the early seventies. Sonora Webster Carver,
blinded by a dive in 1931, was the most famous diver.
The details concerning Donald Trump are also true.*

Pearl divers are greased lightning, coated all over
with some kind of lube that flashes them down,
rocks in their hands to sink them deeper, faster,

a hundred feet in one breath. Bet they stop thinking,
their names dissolving in the Indian Ocean, the Persian Gulf,
linked up like fish stitching the flow with silver.

Oyster beds lie hidden in plain sight,
some oysters crying tears that never dry,
nacre to wash away something that interferes,

like getting something in your eye. The divers' burglary
is in the sway of things down there where teeth gleam,
fingers reaching for the bead in oyster plush,

stashing pearls like the tooth fairy bagging milk teeth
from under pillows. At least she leaves coins.
People say the taste of oysters makes you hungry for love..

But I bet it's the same for them, anyway - the real pearl
is the moment you curl like a wave, unborn again,
glued to Pegasus in flight whose wings vibrate

right through you, stirring air you forget to breathe.
When I went down with both eyes open, the time
I lost my sight, maybe I was trying to see those wings

I'd felt so many times. Maybe that's not right.
Maybe it was pure bad luck. Anyway, I went blind.
Got so bored I'd shoot you for a nickel, till I dived

again. Dived blind for ten years. Showed I was still
alive. Showed me, my husband, showed the sky,
not so much the crowd below, though they were nice,

- but for the horse and me in flight, it was never about
the audience. Not like that trumped-up Trump-man,
the one who bought the Steel Pier in Atlantic City,

in the nineties, long after we were gone, tried to do
a Diving Mule routine to pack them in again. Cruel,
sending the mule down alone, no rider, then a dog

or two. No dog dives unless it's right off the bank
for a swim - or for a rescue, they'd do anything,
not that Trumper would know jack about that. Anyway,

Animal Rights got it right for once, with Trumpingbrat.
He's done with diving mules. Bet he's got a trick or two
stowed up those sleeves. Doc Carver would know,

worked every rodeo, watched all the snake-oil hypnotists
match the gleam in their eyes to their teeth and cufflinks.
Doc started up the Diving Horse when his horse jumped

into the Platte River, Nebraska,1881. *Never thought a horse
could do that,* he said. Ask me, that horse didn't have
a whole fat lot of choice, seeing how the bridge was down.

Maybe we none of us choose much. He signed me on, trained me
up on Lightning. Then Red Lips and me got going. Reckon
I'll join him under that Winesap soon. Ninety-nine. Time

to take a dive, like boxers do. Throw the fight. Best apple there is,
a Winesap. Horses love the bite. Used to straddle that top branch,
Red Lips nickering to me under the tree. Some horses are natural

people-whisperers, not all. Got my nerve back after I went blind,
climbing the Winesap in the dark, listening to him underneath.
Might do it again, some rainy night. Sometimes I still hear

that boiling chuckle from Red Lips. Time for another dive –
but then again, with my luck I'd just lie there in a mess,
survive. Can't risk it for the folks I've got left,

can I? Maybe I'll sit tight, let the Winesap blow,
rock my aching bones, forget about tomorrow,
close my eyes, hunch down on Pegasus in flight.

Presolution
Alastair Birch

You are the kind of person that likes to finish crosswords and leave
them for others to find –

you cannot stand the thought of them solving the wrong solution.[1]

Teaching people to think is your greatest joy.

It irritates you that you are the only one that seems to know how.[2]

Tell me, how will you go about surmounting this riddle I am
setting you?[3]

Perhaps every word is a hundred-letter anagram you will never
solve,

white text silently mocking you from behind its colourless veil.[4]

Or perhaps all you need to do is find the right key and put it in the
right door –

and of course you will find them, for who would I write this for if
not for you?[5]

The test begins – all I ask is for you to remember that nobody other
than yourself is setting it.[6]

---

[1] Here we see the poet's admission through the metaphor of a crossword that
everything he or she writes is like a puzzle – which is to say, that each poem has an
intended and objective meaning.
[2] This and the previous line are a call to action directed at the reader, signifying that
they are one of the "chosen few" gifted enough to understand the message and should
do whatever they can to spread it to those less fortunate than themselves.
[3] A explicit verification of the above: I have no further analysis to offer at this stage,
but it is nice to have confirmation that my interpretation is the legitimate one.
[4] Obvious sarcasm daring the reader to look closer– the observer of these footnotes
can be reassured that the document contains nothing written in invisible ink, and
rearranging the letters of the poem into every possible word combination produces
nothing of value.
[5] But how can every potential reader of the poem have the necessary knowledge
required to figure out its message? Clearly the work is directed at someone specific –
but who? There must be a way of knowing: I must try harder.
[6] I have no idea what this means.

Attitude: rampant
Alexander Velky

We fell asleep beneath red leaves
And left the goats to ramble.
I dreamt of apple blossom,
You dreamt of apple crumble;
I type all this into my phone
And fruit becomes computer.
I filter my photography
To make my dog look cuter,
And all my friends are far away
Now they fit in my pocket;
And every thought's a cliché now
So every second's "fuck it".

We fell asleep beneath bare branches,
Left the goats to ramble.
I touched my palm upon your chest
And felt your ribcage tremble.
I endeavour to express this
Like milk into a pail
But the sentiments turn sour
As in a fairytale.
The boys are crying wolf again
And everyone's afraid;
The stars have fallen from the sky
But all is safe inside.

We fell asleep beneath the blossom,
Left the goats to wander.
I dreamt about a boat at sea,
You dreamt the squalls and thunder;
Washed up on dark desert sand,
We wake up in the future.
Emoting through emojis now,
We've kama for some sutra;
But the best of all our tools

Are blaming us for badness,
And all our fading danger signs
Are wearing thin of redness.

We fell asleep beneath ripe fruits
To caprine rumination.
I woke to find a note that said
You'd left for the train station.
You're working in the city now;
You're working for survival.
I'm living for the love of it,
Awaiting your arrival.
I'll pluck the apples from this bough
When they are good and ready,
And we'll have apple crumble then
If we're still going steady.

Calypso's Island
Antony Mair

When he looked back, it was always summer there:
a breeze from the sea cooled sunlit terraces,
above the vines and swaying corn. Rain fell while they slept.

In Ithaca, the seasons caught him in their dance,
and he shaped his body to their tune, loving his wife
no less for the streaks of silver in her hair. But there were times

he couldn't tell her of, when he traced her bones' fine lines,
and brushed his lips against her temple and felt, under his fingers,
the ghost of the goddess he'd lived with for those seven years,

just as now, after so many years we've been together,
shadows of others still hover in this small bedroom,
our own Ithaca - traces of passions without a future,

buried in the skin, like the scars Penelope
ran her finger-tips across at night, jealous of his past,
and wondering why he'd chosen to return.

Oddbods
Catherine Ayres

We embroider our edges with slow smiles,
tuck ourselves into home-made jumpers
and hide in our mothers' expectations.
We are happiest in the avocado shadow of bathrooms,
turning over sea urchins with trembling hands;
or crouched next to French windows, listening
to a scratched recording of birdsong.
Our guinea pigs are called Monica - they are both boys.
We like our eggs hard boiled, our celery lined with salt.
We *know* how to use a soup spoon.
We do not understand posters; all our clippings
are pinned to floral wallpaper. Our bedrooms
are like conches, delicate and full of whispers.
(It is often hard to leave them).
Laughter clatters round us like knives falling in another room;
we are soft and solemn as Sundays and do not flinch.
One day we will live in the tree on the hill,
hang our horse brasses from its branches.
When our dandelion clocks swim like spiders
towards the moon, we will teach the teddies about Jesus,
serenade the cowpats with our favourite hymns.
It won't matter that our dollies are lonely;
we will draw them close, wipe the tears
from their large, unblinking eyes.

April
Elaine Beckett

We knew about the cemetery
four hundred yards on the left,
and we discussed it –

people die all the time
so they might as well be buried there.

Yet late at night, when we are lying still
on our deep filled mattress,
in the quiet,

I can't help imagining
how close we all are –

and remembering how
weeks before my mother's death,
she justified it by saying she didn't envy me

living on, into the twenty first century,
with all that was likely to happen.

A brave enough thought.
Yet watching these clouds, and the wood pigeon's flight
to the uppermost twig of the tall poplar tree,

and this light that persists,
I've decided never to use such an argument;

I shall miss everything,
every single part of it – the tragedies,
the messiness, even the stupidity.

The End of the End of the Pier Show
Emma Simon

Call it The Titanic Spirit: tonight
we have a show to end all shows,
kicked off by our teenage xylophonist
performing 'Flight of the Bumblebee' blindfold.

Be dazzled as El Niño, East Anglia's premier
flamenco troop perform their showstopper routine —
testament to our unshaken belief
in Victorian riveting, balustrades and glitter balls.

Yes, we have stood by, watched struts
that held up Yarmouth's ice-cream shops erode,
waved goodbye to penny-slot telescopes
sloshed away in last year's high spring tide.

But your tears are now no longer enough
to resalinate the oceans — so tonight
let's raise the roof of the Cromer Pavillon:
Resist the Great Storm Surge!

It may be too late for the Andaman Islands,
but money raised from ticket sales
will help those forced to flee bungalows
on the English Riviera.

And if we become unmoored midway
drift out on this boardwalk ark to darker seas,
don't panic, ladies & gentlemen,
our Michael Barrymore tribute act is first aid trained.

Enjoy our award-winning stage hypnotist.
The house band — the King Canuters —
will play loud and long into the night,
as we sail on, towards uncertain morning.

15

Wisdom's Almanac, or the Science of Sorrel
Geraldine Clarkson

Wisdom is wasted on old wives
Wisdom is wasted on teeth
Wisdom is wasted on owls, and on sphinxes
Wisdom is weighted on the heart
Wisdom is snaked enlightenment, forked
Wisdom is forked enlightenment, snaked
What Wisdom doesn't know could be contained in a hazelnut
A hazelnut contains all of Wisdom, and more
Wisdom is wasted on the hour, on the minute, and on the hoof
Uncomfortably, Wisdom can be wasted on sofas with spiral cushions
and floral borders, with no check
Autumnally, Wisdom can be wasted on stubbled fields
lacking a certain slant of sun
In summer, Wisdom is wasted on batty cricketers and dotty dogs
Wisdom is dearer by amber light through whiskey
and by whiskey through amber light
Wisdom is treasured by hounds, not foxed by folly
Wisdom is beneficial to angels and ambrosial to demons
but nominal for Wisdom Smith & Sophia Loren
Wisdom is wasted on landfill, and wasted on a night out
Wisdom is wasted on those who don't know when to stop
Wisdom is wasted on those who don't know when to start

Wisdom is wasted on those uncertain about the middle
Wisdom is waisted and corseted, belted and buckled
Wisdom bucks the trend for wisdom

Wisdom is brighter than angels' teeth, and lower than humility—more abashed
Wisdom is clearer by night— brasher—and more subtle by day, *musha*
Wisdomware is chic and durable—'All will be well' emblazoned under the glaze
Wisdom is a crack in beauty, and a cracker at a party
Wisdom cricks her neck to see into the next field
In spring, Wisdom is lissom and lithe, blithe, skylark-like, carried on
the broom in the breeze

Wisdom is up to her neck in intrigue and up to her ears in pearls,
which she tosses to the grass
Wisdom makes silver, mud; and mud, silver
as well as silver mud, and mud silver
Wisdom is patient as sorrel soup with thyme
Wisdom is a Methodist preacher who, having left her notes on the bus, finds
her words sprout wings
An aunt of Wisdom's lives in Egypt
Wisdom says 'yes' every time she doesn't say 'maybe' or 'can I help you'
Wisdom has three middle names and none of them is Stanley
Wisdom is a castle in Spain with turquoise-teal mosaics
and onion domes, celery turrets, gourdy walls...
Wisdom is wasdom
Wisdom is a trick practised with a flick of the hand
by the Queen of Diamonds at dusk
Wisdom is wasted on backflipping circus artistes who lose their verve
Wisdom is flipping scintillating, a gigantic beach ball to knead
and get a wiggle on
Latterly Wisdom has been wasted by the wise
and, for the uncertain future, Wisdom *is*, utterly.

Pooh Sticks
Giles L. Turnbull

Walking   by   Birstwith   mill
sluiced   from   the   Nidd,
flowering   now   many   moons   since   cotton,
I   found   my   feet
amongst   memories   of   Dalmatians   and   dustbin   men,
of   sneaking   under   the   hedge
to   lend   a   hand   with   baking   day   pastry.

I   grew   into   an   explorer
bouncing   across   the   bridge   across   the   beck
teeming   with   stickleback;
I   breathed   paper   monsters   into   life
risking   enchantment.

Panini   by   the   Thames
broke   the   hours
and   the   morning   and   evening   tides
of   London   lives   at   the   edge   of   everything
but   with   little   time   to   dive   in.

I   found   wings,
flew   and   landed   by   the   Hooch
walked   the   dog   with   you,
watching   a   bigger   dog   walk   a   bigger   man   across   the   flow.

the   system   played   its   own   games   —
conjurer   of   fusilli   rain
the   lake-effect   weather   of   Buffalo,
vertiginous   snowdrifts   year-on-year
except   the   year   when   everything   melted   and   ran   away

bringing   me   back   to   my   land   of   the   Taff   and   the   Tawe
looping   their   arms   around   the   ribs   of   the   hills,
flowing   like   the   match   day   singing
Hiraeth,   the   unquenchable   sense   of   home;

I still cannot convincingly swim.

Angela Lansbury
Ian Walker

for Bobby

She turned up to help move a three-seater leather sofa, cream.
Wore a superhero inspired outfit – probably not by accident.
Deduced that the feet would need to come off to fit through the doorframe.

Monitored the situation with the wit of a witch-in-training.
She offered to wash the pots. *You dry and put away.*
Sang the verse from Be Our Guest at the top of her magnificent lungs.

Ditched the rubber gloves in favour of pruning her already wrinkled hands.
And once they were done, drank some rum, from a tankard. Love it.
Put on a hat-with-three-corners for sheer whimsy. Lupine company.

Sat down (on the floor – because the sofa was now in the hall)
to break her Murder, She Wrote viewing virginity, glass in hand.
Then, with a wink, fake Maine accent, freeze-framed laugh, she left.

Sometimes, a person is needed more than they know.

Make me a miracle
Jane Wynn

I have prayed for you in many churches
bent my head and sent silent words
God help, God heal, God speed
I have lit candles and sighed at the bold
efficiency of their plastic; smiled
at the waxy proficiency of the real
Mercy you, Mercy me, Mercy all
Here in such vaulted heights surely
a prayer can fly deft as a hawk
and make such a squawk in God's ear
that he can only listen

I have knelt for you in many churches
Slid quietly into their other communion
God save, God send, God heed
Seen mantilla'd madames muttering
Heard cigarette-throated signors
 spluttering, grieving their lengthy losses
Make me, Make you, Make them
Here, where intention makes passion, surely
my thoughts must hit you like a squall of wind
and make such a thrumming in your ear
that you have to hear

I have sent thoughts to you in so many churches
trying to believe because you believed
In *God help, God heal, God speed*
Watched incense drift like morning mist
Seen holy hands lift to the heavens
Mercy you, Mercy Me, Mercy all
In Sciacca's Basilico, in Notre Dame cathedral
In Stavros chapel, in Bruges' Holy Infant Sepulchre
In all these sacred places where life is the lie
I have asked of you, *For God's sake*
Make me a miracle. Send me a sign.

If not for God's sake
Then for mine

Histories
Jeni Williams

1.
Here there is only ash and sparse black grass
the dry rustle of charred branches falling.
The forest of stories consumes itself.

The old monsters, bears and wolves, the hard man
swinging his axe, transforming life to wood:
all gone. Nothing left in the crackling dust.

Smoke chokes the milky breath of history.
No lost birds glint gold on the soughing bough
singing lost mothers back from mantled graves,

Though bees gather the sweetness of roses
no one can conjure honey from the air.
Straw cannot be spun to gold. Never could.

Icy fear inhabits this forest; fear
and ghosts. Maybe nothing ever changes,
and it was always the same: so accept

the cold histories of ash, forget pain
forget memories of before. And yet

ice forms on forest floors and thick snows fall:
we will die without the warmth of stories.

2.
There is nothing natural in stasis,
silence, or the slow progression of ice.

3.
A girl and a beast in the old stories,
a man and a bird, a man and a fish,
or a wolf and a girl, a bear-maiden:
the shedding of skins in revelation.
Each risks all to encounter difference.

A man and an underwater brightness
clasped fierce and glistening, held on firm land.
Her long hair like a gown of shining green
cloaks her slim white limbs as the frost stars fall.

Her fish sisters twist in terror, turning
quick grey pewter in the churning air.

4.
The soft seal woman slides on the ice pack,
wary of her bear lovers, beautiful.
A dancing girl with melting kohl rimmed eyes,
surfaces to the bitter-cold salt air;

to white and white, to towers of blue ice,
to shining white and bluer shadows, to
the sharp cracks of fissured glacial floes
crashing through the slurry of icy seas.

When she sings her voice is so thin and high
her song erects icicle palaces.
Her ice breath shivers to mist, to mirrors
that reflect her dark eyes and the pale sky,
that strip her of excess, hold and contain
her cold brilliance in a fine clear line.

She sings and her supple skin falls away:
a gold kimono lit in arctic light.
The gleaming silk slips off, her hair hangs loose,

a silver girl steps forward, small, weightless,
on naked feet, into the tremulous
sharp sensitivity of the human,

She sings her being to white brittleness.
Her new self shines in glassy shards of cold,
her new skin so baby smooth she cannot
touch herself for wonder. She is so clean.
She smells nothing but clarity and space.

And downwards through the air the white birds fly.
Clothes spun from starlight drop over her head;
they lift her up, into the singing sky.

Her fish brothers, astonished, leap to see:
the far-away bear lifts his head and howls;
a puzzled whale breaches the ice and gasps:
as she rises his spout falls in crystals.

5.
Below her bird flight the old story tells
how a lone figure crosses the white ice,
haunts the frozen seas, spears the frozen dark.

Now, lit by her bright song, he looks up,
harpoon steadied, then a precise whiplash
of stripped sealskin drags the sky flier down.

Her singing freezes to a hail of tears.
She is trapped in her slender grace, keening.
Untouchable silver caught in his grasp.

Now she will be his silent wife, dreaming
of cold, of her lost seal self, aching for
the fish, the birds, the howling bear, the whale.

6.
Yet there is no end to transformation.
Just three strokes will suffice for her to slip
back below her beloved ice. Things change.

Ash may become ink so write this:
    Consider the wonder of old stories,
    the long evolution of enchantment.

then this:
    There is nothing natural in stasis
    or an exquisite extinction in ice.

Parakeet, Christmas Day
John Wilks

You
so unlike our tuneful robin and blackbird
with your alien raucous squawking
coming over here
helping yourself to free berries
sunflower seeds and fatballs
and the crabapple at the top of the tree
which you now balance in one claw
and offer up to red beak curved
like a miniature defiant scimitar

You
uninvited guest
unexpected gift
vibrant emerald green
in our grey midwinter garden
skilful aviator
survival expert
bold as a Brit
you are most welcome here
please don't fuck off back to where you came from!

Deafening
Jonathan Greenhause

Nelson abhors silence. He
collects claxons,
assembles air-conditioning units, punches up

muscle cars,
cruise ships. Nelson revs up his engines,
blasts arias,

taps spoons against metallic countertops,
bangs bangs bangs
on drums, echoes sirens, sets off

car alarms. Nelson
imitates water fowl, splashes in
wading pools,

befriends a pod of dolphins, shrieks
back & forth
with seagulls. He makes farting sounds

with his armpits,
recites famous speeches poems short
& long stories,

tests of the Emergency Broadcasting System.
Nelson bottles
the wrath of hurricanes earthquakes

& volcanoes,
channels the Old Testament God's fury,
wears combat boots.

He can't stand the quiet because of his
intolerable loneliness,
because no one wants to be with someone

as riotous as Nelson.

Babelsburg, 1994
Jonathan Timbers

(Soon to be renamed) *KarlMarxstrasse*,
is splattered with election posters.
One candidate, in a white fedora,
doesn't look like a merchant banker.
In the canteen, an Italian electrician
demonstrates to the French cook
that the *Maxpax* isn't working.
In Herr Direktor's office, Reifenstahl's agent phones.
History is her diver in the thirty-six
Olympics, who falls whilst a reverse image
of the descent is superimposed
in brilliant black and white: the reflection
of the waves of impact
pulsating like the old *RKO* sign, perhaps,
transmitting from nation to nation.

Breaking Point
Louisa Adjoa Parker

Written as part of a collaboration with Josephine Corcoran for the Enemies Project

I Breaking

Bones break, then slowly knit
together. Skulls fold in upon
themselves when smashed. Bone china,
glass, when dropped, splits from a whole
into immeasurable pieces.
Hearts break, then mend, and break
again. News breaks in red
across our TV screens. Waves break
on our shores. Breaking – to come apart,
to split the way our country did –
into two sharp-edged halves
like a plate dropped on the floor.

II Point

A conversation has a point, or not.
The tip of a pencil, scrawled on a ballot slip
has a point until it's blunted.
Campaigns have a point, sometimes.
Or they are run by pointless fools
with bad hair days and rubber smiles
who don't expect to win, then walk away,
leave us picking up the pieces
of ourselves, littering the ground
like broken glass, watching
as they catch the light.

Returning to Woods on a Snowy Evening
Mark D. Cooper

Developers have sought permission for
much-needed housing. Many trees are gone.
Although I've rarely walked in them before,
these woods belong to me, if anyone.

My new coat covers something old in me,
a looker-at-birches who journeyed on.
Ice storms silver everything here but time.
Diggers crouch: eager to do and be done.

Trees are like flagpoles beside the road,
marking the quiet border of a ceasefire.
At 1 a.m., I've come out here to tread
down snow and put the freeze on my desire.

Love, in any language, can't be understood.
The call's been made, the council has agreed.
No one can say how dark, how deep this wood.
How long before suburbs become its seed.

The Myth of the Myth of Sisyphus
Mark Fiddes

The lad reads Camus like Sisyphus,
every Penguin page so inclined
that the meaning might roll back
with a groan into his rubble brain.
He says truth's just a bigger boulder,
harder to shoulder, shape or throw,
gathering speed but no moss...

(moss)
which older men should mould
as a felten hat to cool their brains
or sport as a velveteen jacket to dine
in places with strict dress codes
so that they may complain about
the dreadful amount of piss
the ruling class leave on the loo seat...

(loo seat)
the last porcelain bastion of thought
on the digital plains of distraction
where cats battle it out with cakes,
side-boobs and Presidential candidates
as sweaty and opinonated as crusaders
waving their many pouted Selfies
like Madonnas...

(Madonna)
whose cult is overdue a comeback,
- Joseph's wife, not Guy Ritchie's -
to be venerated with roadside shrines
by bus stops, piled with stone cairns
showing how far our myths have come
since Sisyphus, Prometheus and
that fire the Gods still want back.

Shed Travel / *working from home*
Michael Fitzgerald

the joy of eating biscuits; don't expect it to continue
after you have eaten them
just saying
I fall ill by my own hand on occasion

my search for the bleakest home on earth
is in full swing...added to favorites
my abandoned soviet housing block
if they'll let me in

I can talk better without this smoke
dusting my chords
but who would want such a miserable bastard
articulating his thoughts

tapping out this invoice
I'm due to meet the king
somebody get me out of here
I'll do anything

I was up high, then down real low
everything is moving
way too slow
Jesus only made it to thirty three or so

Early Doors
Michael Woods

This was when to catch him in good spirits -
before the mid-evening rush and jostle,
before the calling for another bottle,
another pint, with hardly time to fill it.
Now he had the time to pass the time of day.
While the unwatched clock cut him some slack
he smoked, talked and joked as he topped up black,
patient porter. *Liffey water*, some would say.
Don knew better, ignored their ignorance
of the Wicklow mountain source. What is true
doesn't always go down well. Circumstance
dictates that knowledge benefits the few.
He set his clock – ten minutes ahead. Dead
on eleven he'd call time. Enough said.

Spitfire Kitchen
Samantha Wynne-Rhydderch

English Rose they called it when my Gran put this kitchen in
after the war. Made by the chaps who built Spitfires
with spare aircraft grade aluminium, they diversified
into double drainers and splashbacks. A flamerino
was no longer a Spit whining into the Channel in a fireball
after 93 sorties out of Biggin Hill but something between
a flambée and a meringue. They always said
your uncle brought a light touch to the controls
from playing the piano; how towing a plume of smoke

he knew he'd never make the aerodrome so he skirted
the tennis courts, Deal parish hall and the potatoes
on Ted's allotment to slice through the ragwort
surprising six sheep and the farmer who went to
put the kettle on. Get into the port side wing
of your Spitfire kitchen. Turn both magnetos on.
Propellor into forward pitch. Open the throttle. Check
trim, rudder, flaps. Let's get this kitchen in the air.

Flight
Sarah Diamond

A bomb went off somewhere
I felt it like a tremor, like waking from a dream
and we evacuated.

Was the flight cancelled?
You went to search the runway
and I could see on the horizon
our waiting plane, the steps leading
up.

I stayed behind
in the little flat with the mother and daughter
who smiled like twins and wrapped their arms
around themselves, two Russian dolls.

I watched you leave me
descend the metal staircase
until you started to trip and fall
and land on the ground
then disappear.

I ran to you
in the too-slow movement of a nightmare
searching for your body
a pale plume from a plant's insides
a porous softness that I gathered
to ignite by blowing
as I'd seen men do to light a fire.

I tried to rekindle
To enflame you.

And my heart is as pale as winter birds
yearning to take flight.

That hot summer
Sarah Doyle

we were mermaids. Our skin was salt-glistened,
slick. Legs fused into piscine tails, and residual

memories of walking receded with each tide-turn.
Newly gilled, we stayed under for hours, spooling

s-shapes over and over. Sometimes we surfaced
to haunt rock pools, poring over the sea's discarded

spoils. Faces immersed, we sucked in trapped sprats,
relishing the salinity on our greedy tongues, our teeth

picked clean with ruined crab-claws as we wallowed
in our fishiness. We were untamed, all tangled hair

and shining eyes. Our language was guttural, secret –
all we needed, ululating into the vinegar-sharp air,

proclaiming dominion over sea-anemones, amber,
samphire, driftwood, starfish, belemnites, limpets.

Whelk-shells were garlanded, primitive amulets
worn to ward off September: its uniforms, its shoes,

its rules.

Rebel / Cause
Shauna Robertson

And so this little old lady (I hate that term but in this case it's true
since she can't be more than four feet and looks about ninety)
sucks hard on her Dunhill and says it wasn't the Porsche Spyder
that killed him at all in fact he didn't even own it at that point
having bet it in a card game a month or so before and lost
but of course when he died they had to prize it back
from her son Rudy (God rest his soul) who'd won the hand,
so they could stage the whole story for the press and the fans
to look like a rebel's exit since the real exit was so unremarkable
it didn't even make the local rag.

                         It was just one of those
unlucky things. He was in a roadside diner on route 466
near Paso Robles and ordered a chicken sandwich which
must've had a bone in it because he started to cough and splutter
but it wasn't the chicken bone either since his buddy Rolf clapped
him on the back and it shot out right away, but just as it did
poor Jimmy slumped forward and his face landed smack
on the formica tabletop and that was the last time
anybody saw him breathe. Heart, apparently.
Or someplace else to be.

But For The Trees
Sue Rose

I struggle
with the ancient dialect
of the wood — the way
these branches, lying
where they fell in shallows,
seem to form a rune
that articulates the hook,
the hunt, the elusive fish
wary in the stir of water
shirring over stone;
        I'm searching
for sense, a way to belong
in these alien spaces
but, like the Hebrew letters
I struggled to learn,
these sodden logs that touch
in one place only, signify
something more than shape
when they reach
for each other, mute
as the black script
of the Torah.
           I stop at the edge
of the ford and peer
into idle water. I doubt
that fish slip like brume
through these narrows
but, if they did,
I would not know
their names.

When you're having a dream about flying
but your accountant shows up
Susannah Dickey

The night I can't sleep I lie with one foot turning circles off the edge of the bed.
The other is floating with no control in a rotoscope-video half-dream; the sort
that always tricks me. My thoughts are legs, trying to run in a swimming pool.

We are standing in an empty subway train, the interior the same tentative pink
of old NHS prescription glasses, the type my grandmother still wears. The image
of her jerks on my mind like a fishing line and I ask you to distract me.

The different carriages are like links in a sausage chain. There is spongy, ground
meat padding on the seats and a smell of warm moisture. If I could touch the
atmosphere I think it would feel raw. A doughy abdomen. A body, post-sex.

You suggest we play hide and seek. There is nowhere to hide in here but you
stand for a while with your eyes closed. If the train moved you might fall. Even if
it didn't move, you might fall, so I don't move, just in case. I could reach the end

of the train in one minute, but I don't want to risk not existing in your immediate
pouch of time. When I went away last summer you were suddenly an hour
behind; your pain installed in history. I couldn't fix it, and I want to fix it.

You open your eyes and I am there, lurking ineffectually behind a silver pole. You
know instantly that I'm thinking of a Scooby-Doo episode and we dissolve into
laughs that echo all the way to the one-minute time delay at the end of the line.

We look at each other in the reflection of the pole - I think that even a caricature
of you would be beautiful. The colours start to merge and blur in a whirlpool and
I place the blame on that other obstinate foot, suspended in space, rotating.

I half-wake in the cold air and I feel as if I've been planted in soil. We are in the
same time zone but you are further away than four carriages, somewhere I can't
touch. I close my eyes to see us taking the 15-second plunge from link to link.

We leave 15 second ago *us*, peeking round a funhouse mirror one-inch thick, giggling, and we become 15 second from now *us*, my hands on your chest and your face pressed against mine - a flipbook inevitably that terrifies me.

Hours later we are still wandering up and down the train; the air is thinning and we ignore the subtle change in your hair colour, or the deepening tracks between my eyebrows. You say 'Funny how immersion therapy doesn't seem to work'.

After our hundredth oscillation my grandmother appears. Her skin is like the easy-tear underside of a baby hedgehog. Her husband died and now she sits and fidgets with her plastic exoskeleton glasses, existing in one-minute intervals.

I say to you, if this were a bad short film or short story now I would realise that *that* is actually me; that I end up alone and bitter and undercooked looking. You squeeze my hand tighter and say 'That would be cruel, if any of this were real.'

LIVE CANON